ARTIST AND COLOURMAN

Common Councilman: W. J. Reeves Esq. (Water-colour. c. 1820)

ARTIST
AND
COLOURMAN

by
Michael Goodwin

Published by
Michael Goodwin
for Reeves
on the occasion
of their
200th anniversary

by the same author
NINETEENTH CENTURY OPINION

for Alison

First published in 1966
© Reeves and Sons Ltd.,
Lincoln Road, Enfield,
Middlesex, 1966
Printed in Great Britain
Partridge & Love, Bristol

Foreword

THERE ARE a number of firms in Great Britain who have traded for more than two centuries and although the history of Reeves is available in considerable detail it is likely to follow the pattern of other old established businesses, and become of chief interest to members of the family and staff alone.

In the small but specialised trade of artist colourman it was felt that an effort should be made to break away from the purely internal chronicles of the firm. To this end Mr Michael Goodwin was given the task of writing to a somewhat broader brief.

This I feel he has successfully achieved, by producing an interesting picture of the interplay between the changing needs of the artist or student, and the response to those needs by the artist colourman, while throughout the pages runs the thread of the history of the House of Reeves.

Brian D. Wild

CHAIRMAN

[v]

Illustrations

Common Councilman: W. J. Reeves Esq. (artist unknown).
Water-colour. Reeves Collection   *frontispiece*

facing page

The 'Weierhaus', by Albrecht Dürer. c. 1496.
*Water-colour. Reproduced by courtesy of the Trustees of the
British Museum*   16

'One of their Religious Men', by John White. c. 1585
*Water-colour. Reproduced by courtesy of the Trustees of the
British Museum*   17

A Wayside Inn, by Paul Sandby. c. 1772
*Water-colour. Reproduced by courtesy of the Trustees of the
British Museum*   24

Durham Cathedral, by Thomas Hearne. 1783
*Water-colour. Reproduced by courtesy of the Victoria & Albert
Museum*   25

Isaac Smith's paint box   28

Botany Bay. c. 1770   29

The Royal Warrant. 1790   29

The Villa d'Este, by J. R. Cozens. c. 1780–90
*Water-colour. Reproduced by courtesy of the Victoria & Albert
Museum*   32

Kirkstall Abbey, by Thomas Girtin. c. 1801
*Water-Colour. Reproduced by courtesy of the Victoria & Albert
Museum*   33

Early Reeves Trade Card. c. 1770   36

The Greater Silver Palette. 1781   37

Europe a Prophecy, by William Blake. 1794
*Water-colour. Reproduced by courtesy of the Trustees of the
British Museum*   44

In a Shoreham Garden, by Samuel Palmer. c. 1829
*Water-colour. Reproduced by courtesy of the Victoria & Albert
Museum*   45

Water-front at Benares, by Thomas Daniell. c. 1790
Water-colour. Reproduced by courtesy of the Secretary of State   *between pages*
for Commonwealth Relations   48—49

St. Anne's Hill, by J. M. W. Turner. c. 1830
*Water-colour. Reproduced by courtesy of the Trustees of the
British Museum*   48—49

Petworth House interiors, by J. M. W. Turner. c. 1830
*Water-colours. Reproduced by courtesy of the Trustees of the
British Museum*   48—49

Rocky Landscape—Sunset, by J. S. Cotman. c. 1835–9
*Water-colour. Reproduced by courtesy of the Victoria & Albert
Museum*   48—49

Introduction

AS A PUBLISHER I have acted as midwife to countless business histories. These have ranged from full-scale works, running to some six or seven hundred pages, to extended essays like the present one. With few exceptions the most lively and interesting of these have been written not in the form of a purely domestic account of a company's history, but within the framework of outside events. In this way a company's contribution to the community it serves emerges far more significantly than when its activities are regarded merely in isolation.

I would like to record my thanks to the board of directors of Messrs Reeves & Sons for the freedom they have allowed me to exercise in my approach to their history. Theirs has been a most enlightened attitude.

I have also to thank Mr Brian Little, whose previous work in this field revealed a number of hitherto unknown facts about the early history of Reeves, of which with his permission I have freely availed myself.

Finally, acknowledgments are due to the following authorities to whom I have had resort for some of the early background material:

MATERIALS OF THE ARTIST, *M. Dörner*, George G. Harrap & Co. Ltd., 1935

A HISTORY OF WATER-COLOUR PAINTING IN ENGLAND, *Gilbert R. Redgrave*, Sampson Low, Marston and Company Ltd., 1892

ENGLISH WATER-COLOURS, *Laurence Binyon*, C. H. Adam & Charles Black, 1944

ART AND THE CHILD, *Marion Richardson*, University of London Press, 1948

A HISTORY OF BRITISH WATER COLOUR PAINTING, *H. M. Cundall, I.S.O., F.S.A.*, B. T. Batsford Ltd., 1929

THE PAINTER'S WORKSHOP, *W. G. Constable*, Oxford University Press, 1954

ARTISTS AND THEIR FRIENDS IN ENGLAND, VOL. II, 1700–1799, *William Whitley*, The Medici Society, 1928

MICHAEL GOODWIN

Artist and Colourman

THERE IS A BULK OF LITERATURE ON THE ART AND exponents of water-colour painting. Numerous references exist to the materials employed by watercolourists from the earliest times. The artists' colourmen alone have not received the attention they deserve. It is to their researches, experiments and progressive achievements that the refinement of technique and the spread of activity in water-colour painting since the closing decades of the eighteenth century have been so largely due. Pre-eminent among these colourmen were the Reeves. This year the firm of Reeves and Sons celebrates its bi-centenary.

To assess their contribution from the outset it is helpful to have some knowledge of earlier traditions and materials. Water-colour is not only one of the most widely used processes; it is one of the oldest. The earliest form of water-colour painting was tempera. It was practised by the Egyptians as long ago as 3000 B.C. in the execution of papyrus and wall-based paintings, the colours being mixed with water and fixed with a medium composed of mastic, wax, and various glues. The technique was transmitted in turn to the Greeks, the

Romans, the Byzantines, and to the rest of Europe, reaching England through the instrumentation of itinerant monks. It survived, subject to progressive modifications, through the age of the missal-painters and illuminators to the miniaturists of the Tudor and Elizabethan periods and beyond.

In the Middle Ages the standard medium with which the pigments were mixed for manuscript illumination was *glair*, or white of egg; thereafter gum arabic, derived from the acacia, with the addition of a little honey, sugar or glycerine for greater elasticity, was the medium generally used.

A characteristic of tempera painting is the admixture of white, or some other opaque substance, in the original preparation to prevent the transmission of light from the ground. It was this that probably gave rise to the term 'painting in body colour' which later gained currency. Another characteristic is the thickness with which the colours are applied to the surface, or 'support', more in the manner of oil painting. A form of tempera painting, more commonly called *gouache*, was still practised on the Continent as late as the seventeenth and eighteenth century.

It was the desire for more brilliancy and luminosity that led painters to an increasing economy in the use of white and a greater reliance on transparent colours. Initially, the change was neither rapid nor wholesale, but when and where it occurred it marked the turning point between an ancient tradition and what is now the generally accepted meaning of 'water-colour painting'. A measure of white was still employed, but with discrimination, the object being to render a greater equality of tone and, where required, more substance than is obtainable from pure washes of transparent pigments. At the same time painters found a new delight in the relative freedom with which transparent pigments could be handled.

A passage relating to a series of miniatures attributed to Samuel Cooper, but thought by some to be the work of

Thomas Flatman, another seventeenth century painter, is interesting as revealing not only the discriminatory use of opaque white and transparent colour, but also the method of the artist. All the paintings are made on thin sheets of cardboard. 'The outline was first suggestively sketched, and then the smooth surface of the card under the flesh was covered with a thin wash of opaque white, which, as he used it, must have been an excellent pigment, as it has not changed in any instance. Then with a brownish lake tint the features have been most delicately and beautifully drawn in, and the broad shades under the eyebrows, the nose, and the chin have been washed in flatly with the same tint. This seems to have completed the first sitting. In the next, the painter put in the local colour of the hair, washing in at the same time its points of relief or union with the background, in many cases adding a little white to his transparent colour to make the hue absorbent, and to give it a slight solidity. The shadows of the hair were then hatched in, and the features, and face, in succeeding sittings, hatched or stippled into roundness. Finally the colours of the dress were washed in, in some cases transparently, in others with a slight admixture of white, and the shadows of the dress were given with the local colours of the shadows'.

Following the Reformation, with the loss of the Church's patronage, and the Puritan assault on the arts, continuity had for a time been broken, the limners, or miniaturists, being almost the only practitioners of the pictorial art. The resumption came with the seventeenth century figure-painters of 'history' subjects. At the same period there was considerable activity on the Continent, notably in the Netherlands, the results of which were to have a marked influence on English painters.

Of the great European masters Albrecht Dürer had been the first to apply himself to water-colour landscape drawing;

there followed Rubens and his pupil Van Dyck, whose style was to be evident in the drawings of Gainsborough, and later in the century Adrian van Ostade. The art of water-colour landscape painting was introduced into England through the works of these and many others. But while their influence was unquestionable they are not the admitted forerunners of the English water-colour tradition. Two other strands in the ultimate development of this tradition are represented by the draughtsmen, who accompanied so many foreign expeditions bringing back with them illustrated records of newly discovered places, and the so-called topographical painters.

The work of one of the earliest English draughtsmen, John White, is recalled by Laurence Binyon in his classic book *English Water-Colours*, published during the last war. In 1585, White accompanied Sir Walter Raleigh on his celebrated voyage to North America. Binyon describes his water-colour drawings, many of which were later purchased by the British Museum, as having 'a genuine merit, a sensitive quality, of their own' despite the fact that they were not executed with an artistic purpose, but to record and give information; as showing 'little restriction in the range of colour, which is applied directly with no grey under-painting'. (Later, both Turner and Girtin began by using the technique of grey under-wash, like the topographical artists of their day, before abandoning it for effects of greater transparency). White's pigments were, of course, less finely ground, his washes less transparent than in later art, but, writes Binyon, 'his method and use of his materials are much the same as Dürer's in his water-colour landscapes'.

Some distinctions need to be drawn when one comes to the topographical tradition. While one cannot positively separate the draughtsman from the topographer—in effect, the interest aroused about the middle of the eighteenth century in antiquarian researches and architectural remains created employment as topographers for many who had hitherto regarded themselves as draughtsmen—the average topographer was subject to a much more austere discipline than, say a man like John White. His imagination was granted no licence; he was usually the servant of the engraver, who followed him; and the bulk of his work was destined to end up in black and white reproduction.

The virtues required of him were fidelity for detail, and precision. Much of his work consisted of outline drawings of buildings and architectural features, the treatment of foliage and landscape conforming to a somewhat mechanical pattern. Light and shade were indicated in grey or sepia Indian ink, the two colours being also used to heighten the perspectives. Later, simple washes of local colour were used, and the outline was either 'worked out' or accentuated with a reed-pen. These were the 'stained' drawings on an Indian ink foundation which were so commonly held to be the direct precursors of the English water-colour school though many, including Laurence Binyon, would disagree on the grounds that such a theory excludes proper recognition of the influence both of the figure-painters, and most especially Rowlandson, and the work of contemporary Continental artists.

The early topographers did, however, give a lead to that notable tradition of water-colour landscape painting based on topography, traceable in a continuous line from the Bohemian painter, Wenzel Hollar, who came to England in 1635, and his friend Francis Place, through Samuel Scott and the Sandbys, Rooker, Hearne, and Dayes, to Girtin and Turner. It is interesting that the Sandbys should have started their careers as military draughtsmen for it has been said that the art of landscape painting in China grew out of the practise of military map-making. Edward Dayes was also a topographical draughtsman, as well as a painter, and his description of the accepted method of laying on the colours in the different parts of the drawing is instructive as revealing the near-transitional stage between the higher development of the topographer's art, and water-colour painting. 'The shadows and middle tints, he tells us, should be made with Prussian blue and a brown Indian ink, the sky with "Prussian blue rather tender", the shades of the clouds with Prussian blue and Indian ink, and he advises working forward from the distance into the foreground, leaving out the blue in the advance, until the foreground is reached, which is to be worked with brown Indian ink only. Finally, the darker parts of the foreground are to be retouched with Vandyke brown.'

It might not be possible to forget for a moment Laurence Binyon's valid objections—as well as a host of exceptions disconcertingly placed in time to the practise of working consistently in a standard range of colours, with or without grey under-painting, in transparent or opaque colour but never in both at once. Nevertheless, the conception of the 'topographical' source of inspiration for the advance from drawing to painting, more particularly from the convention of tinting over a monochrome foundation to direct painting in colour, might be readily acceptable. For, in the strictest interpretation, the 'water-colour drawing' has as its predominant feature the drawing, the paint being employed as a tint; in 'water-colour painting' the value of the underlying drawing is diminished, the paint having precedence in the manner of oil painting. The advance has all the appearance of logicality.

The supreme, acknowledged school of English water-colour painters emerged about 1770, heralded in time at least by John Robert Cozens, whom Turner called 'the greatest genius who ever touched landscape', and maintained its full impetus until well into the nineteenth century. From Cozens to Copley Fielding the period was one of unrivalled achievement in an art which, consequently, came to be known by many as 'the English art'. Its advent, if we are to accept the words of Paul

Sandby's biographer, coincided nearly enough in time with the birth of a new concern for the inadequacy of artists' materials.

By the middle of the eighteenth century the English oil painters could be said to be reasonably well catered for by a number of 'oil and colour men' who dealt in artists' materials as well as in household paints. It is true that their oil colours were of a composition which allowed them to go excessively dry; also that, being sold in little bladders, tied at the top so as to form tiny bags, the paint was apt to be spilled, while that which remained kept badly—a situation which was only ultimately remedied by the introduction of the collapsible metal tube. Nonetheless theirs was a far happier position than that of the painter in water-colours. Until quite late in the century he was handicapped both by the limited range of pigments at his command, and the poorness of their preparation. Paul Sandby was very troubled about the 'poverty of his palette' and went to no little effort to extend and reform it. His biographer writes: 'For many years after Mr. Sandby commenced landscape drawing no colours were in general use except such as were peculiarly adapted for the staining of maps and plans, and indeed it was himself who set Middleton the colour maker to prepare them in somewhat like their present state, and which are now brought to so great perfection by Reeves, Newman and others'. Middleton, it must be said, was rapidly outshone by the firm of Reeves.

The Reeves were heirs to a situation in which so indifferent were the wares of the commercial colourmen, as regards the quality of their pigments and the manner of their preparation, that artists felt almost obliged to prepare their own colours, despite their comparative lack of knowledge of their chemical properties and the time required, which they could ill afford, to grind and treat the pigments—in consequence of which even the more talented frequently courted failure.

[15]

The Reeves unique contribution to this dilemma was the invention of the water-colour cake. How much of a godsend this invention proved to be may best be imagined by recourse to the *Art of Drawing and Painting in Water-Colours*, published in 1770, in which the writer having stated that colours may be distinguished as follows: white, yellow, orange, red, purple, blue, and black—goes into the minutest details as to how the artist should set about preparing them from a variety of roots, and mineral and other compounds, proceeding even so far as to direct him to the druggists and herbalists from whom they might be bought in their raw state. While if any indication were needed of the haphazard and hitherto unscientific approach to the subject of colour making, the following 'grand discovery' of Paul Sandby's should more than suffice: 'A few weeks ago,' he writes to a friend, 'I had a French brick for breakfast: the crust was much burnt in the baking. I scraped off the black, and ground it with gum-water: it produced an excellent warm black colour like mummy, and bears out with great vigour. . . . The day after this discovery I had pork and peas-pudding for dinner. I tried some split peas in the evening in a shovel over the fire, and parched them quite black. This also answers well, very dark and warm, not opaque like ivory black: you will, I know, thank me when you try it, and throw your Indian ink aside.'

The first extant public intimation that the Reeves, initially the brothers William and Thomas, were established in business belongs to an advertisement in the *Morning Herald* of December 31st, 1782. 'Upwards of forty neat colours', it read, were available on sale to all those who were engaged in the painting of miniatures, portraits, maps, and landscapes. It would be interesting to know what these colours were, although it is certain that many of them would be unfamiliar to modern artists. At the turn of the century Ackermann offered the student some sixty or seventy colours, a large number of

The 'Weierhaus', (the little house on the island is also to be seen in the painter's *The Virgin with a Monkey*.) Albrecht Dürer (*Water-colour. c. 1496.*)

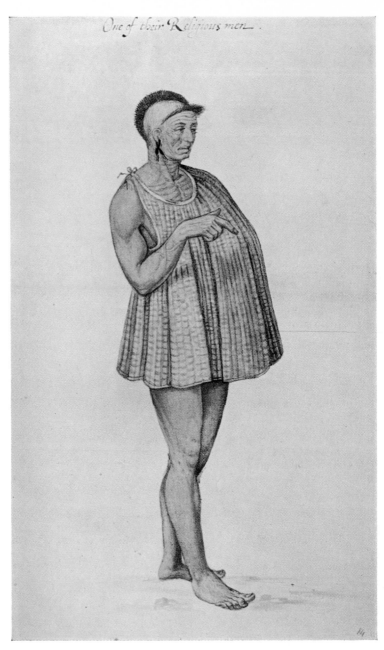

'One of their Religious men'. From the North American drawings of John White (Water-colour. c. 1585)

which were later abandoned because of their non-permanence or lack of depth or brightness, among which notable absentees were cobalt, the cadmiums, rose and brown madder.

Three years after the appearance of the advertisement in the *Morning Herald* the brothers quarrelled and parted. The nature of their disagreement belongs to a later part of the story. All the evidence suggests that their partnership had survived for close on twenty years. William asserted at the time that he had already 'devoted twenty-two years to preparing super fine water-colours, in cakes'. It is unlikely that much of this time would have been taken up with experimentation unsupported by commercial practice. Everything points to the year 1766 as being the date of the brothers' entry into the colour-making business, after which it is probable that for many years they dealt in the numerous requisites of the oil painter and in the earlier, more orthodox range of water-colours. Thomas Reeves would then have been thirty, his brother William twenty-seven. Their father had been a wiredrawer and a member of the Gold and Silver Wiredrawers Company; both were educated at Christ's Hospital; William was later apprenticed to a goldsmith, Thomas, like his father, to a wiredrawer. Each abandoned his craft but no records exist to tell us precisely when. The water-colour cake to which William refers was undoubtedly their invention, an invention which was to open up a whole new horizon for professional and amateur painters alike.

The Reeves cake was a small, rectangular block, more economical to use than anything previously marketed, and the chemical composition of the pigments employed was markedly an improvement on those of existing products. It was not, however, until some time later than their original introduction, as a result of numerous experiments and the trial inclusion of such hygroscopics as honey, that the cakes passed the final test and could be relied upon to keep for long

[17]

periods in a paint box. Meanwhile, the innovation had in itself precipitated a new vogue for water-colour painting, especially among amateurs, who revelled in the simplicity of the new order of materials and in the greater refinement they afforded in the more delicate application of washes. Many imitators reached the market but Reeves appear to have forged ahead.

The greyhound mark which distinguished their early cakes, adopted by the Reeves as crest and trade mark from the arms of a Dorset family named Ryves with whom they claimed a connection, grew steadily in popularity in the last two decades of the eighteenth century.

In 1780, two years before their advertisement in the *Morning Herald*, the brother Reeves submitted to the Society (later the Royal Society) of Arts a 'sample of bistre prepared for super-fine colours'. The Society, whose terms of reference extended beyond the arts, to commerce and industry, was in the habit of awarding premiums for deserving new developments, and had already done so in respect of the discovery in England of cobalt and madder, from which the dyers and clothmakers profited with the makers of paint. The samples, formed in cakes like Indian ink and made up in several colours, were passed for consideration to the Chemistry Committee of the Society. The brothers were summoned and, in the course of interrogation, stated that they had been working on the samples for about three months and that they were satisfied that they would prove cheaper than those 'prepared in common' since they would 'go much further and be good to the last piece'.

The Committee sent the colours for practical tests to three selected artists: Mary Black, a portrait painter and copyist who had exhibited at the Society's exhibitions; Hendrik de Meyer, a Dutch landscape painter who had settled in England and had exhibited at the Academy; and Thomas Hearne, formerly an apprentice of William Woollett, the engraver, and a topographical water-colourist of considerable repute.

In her report, Miss Black declared that the colours were 'very useful' but somewhat hard, and that they might be improved by the addition of 'gum bouge and sap green' (*gamboge* is a vegetable pigment in the yellow colour range, *sap green* a mixed colour; both are impermanent but like many other impermanent colours frequently used for their charming effect). Meyer also commended them for their 'usefulness', particularly 'on travels or voyages'. Hearne was the most enthusiastic, declaring that in his opinion most of the colours were better 'both for convenience and use than any I have before met with'. The committee recommended that Messrs. Reeves should be awarded the Greater Silver Palette 'as a mark of approbation of their method of preparing pigments for painting in Water-Colours'. Duly, on April 11th, 1781, the award was made and the palette has remained to this day in the proud possession of the firm of Reeves.

Soon after gaining this mark of recognition the Reeves, as suppliers of materials to George III and his children, all keen amateur water-colourists, were able to add the Royal Arms to their already existing trade sign—a Blue coat boy, derived, no doubt, from the fact that both brothers had been boys at Christ's Hospital.

Among the relics preserved by Reeves and Sons is a simple, hand-made, wooden colour box containing a set of Reeves cakes and other materials. It is interesting as lending further support to the suggestion that one or other, or both brothers marketed a cake of an earlier form quite some time before the advertisement in the *Morning Herald*. It is romantic because of its particular association with a famous voyage of discovery, echoing the exploits of Sir Walter Raleigh and his talented draughtsman, John White, almost two hundred years earlier.

The box was a gift to the firm from an elderly clergyman, who had inherited it from his great uncle, Isaac Smith, who had retired from the sea as a Rear Admiral to end his days at Merton Abbey, in Surrey. As a young midshipman, Isaac Smith had sailed with Captain Cook in H.M.S. *Endeavour* on the first of Cook's great voyages of circumnavigation and discovery. The expedition's official landscape artist was William Hodges, but Smith, who was related to Cook by marriage, was readily spotted for his talent for accurate drawing and survey work and was mainly employed in these occupations. It would appear to be largely due to him that a number of charts, sketches and hand-drawn maps survive from that voyage, among them a particularly fine map of Otaheite in the Pacific, and a chart of Botany Bay where Midshipman Isaac Smith is purported to be the first Englishman to have jumped ashore from the *Endeavour's* boat, in the face of the threatening aboriginals.

In a subsequent voyage, made between 1772 and 1775 with Captain Cook, Smith as Master's Mate in H.M.S. *Resolution* kept a journal which he illustrated with a number of charts and sketches; to this period also belong a collection of water-colour drawings, one rather delightful one depicting two icebergs, or 'ice islands' as the astonished sailors called them, north of the Atlantic ice pack in the southern waters of the Indian Ocean, together with plans of harbours and sketches of some of the Pacific islands, executed in ink outline with applied green and yellow washes. While they cannot claim an artistic merit comparable with those of John White's, Isaac Smith's contributions were significant, taken in context, and especially interesting to us as being the first water-colours extant which one can safely assume to have been painted with Reeves colours.

Gilbert Redgrave assures us, in his *History of Water-Colour Painting*, published in 1892, and it seems only logical to accept his word, that, before the end of the eighteenth century, Reeves colours were in use by the whole fraternity of artists in this country'. Reeves had their competitors, but they were lesser men by far. Doubtless, many of the older and more conservative artists continued to prepare their own colours but, in the face of the sort of testimonials Reeves were receiving, this traditional practice was bound to go. Besides, in the mounting flurry of water-colour activity, with the heightened tempo of achievement which it brought with it, and the demands for materials from a variety of new sources, many of them semi-professional or amateur, some of them travellers and residents overseas, old methods had no chance of survival —nor was there any longer any justification for them.

Reeves potential market at this time may be broadly measured by reference to the growing demand for artists' materials from new as well as from established sources. By the end of the eighteenth century the business of engravers, and their requirements of artists, had increased enormously both in degree and diversity. The recently cultivated taste for antiquarian researches and architectural remains had given additional employment to numerous draughtsmen who, though subject to a rigid discipline imposed by the technical limitations of the engraver's art, had over the years graduated to the ranks of the topographical artists, among whom the tendency to extend the range of their palette was slowly gaining ground. Much the same nature of employment arose from the fashion among noblemen and great landowners of commissioning topographical artists to compose water-colour drawings of their country houses and surrounding landscapes, many of which drawings were later engraved. There was a growing literature of topographical and travel books illustrated with engravings, and the vogue had started for illustrating in the same manner books of a general nature, and even works of fiction.

The great William Blake was, of course, exceptional in that, partly by inclination but more because of pressure of circumstances, he fashioned his books in their entirety, engraving his poetry and illustrations together on copper plates, drawing off impressions at a common printing press, and roughly colouring the sheets with the simplest of pigments—Dutch pink, ochre, and gamboge—which he probably prepared himself. But many distinguished painters were to turn their hands to this form of art work, notably Turner, Angelica Kauffman and Giovanni Cipriani; some, finding the occupation more profitable, neglected their normal practises and devoted themselves almost exclusively to working for publishers.

Mention has already been made of draughtsmen from the sixteenth century accompanying foreign expeditions, and this was to be a recurrent happening from England as well as from Europe. By the latter part of the eighteenth century, however, painters of repute, too, were frequently travelling abroad, either on expeditions, like the Royal Academician, John Webber, who was absent for four years with Captain Cook on his last voyage in 1776, or on missions, like William Alexander who was to be the first keeper of Pictures and Drawings in the British Museum, and Thomas Hickey, both of whom went with Lord Macartney's embassy to China in 1792, or in the company of private gentlemen of rank or substance, like Henry Pars. His Swiss drawings, which were engraved and may be seen in the Print Room of the British Museum, were executed during a journey with Lord Palmerston, who took him through Switzerland and the Tyrol to Rome. Just as John White's drawings of Virginia were a revelation to his countrymen, so Pars's drawings, when exhibited in London in 1771, caused wonderment to those who had no inkling of the grandeur of the high Alps.

To the demand for materials occasioned by such activities as these must be added the exceptional requirements of the building boom of the 1780s and early 1790s in terms of materials for architects and draughtsmen. Besides the manufacture of oil and water-colour paints, Reeves appear to have been particularly concerned to produce a new variety of Indian ink which would further facilitate drawing. As it happened, it was this new departure that signalised the rupture between the two brothers already mentioned.

On February 16th, 1784, Thomas wrote to the Society of Arts, reminding them of the award given to 'his' superfine colours, and enclosing a sample of ink of the 'Indian' type. He called it 'Reeves British ink', and claimed for it that it was equal to the finest from China, and substantially cheaper. The sample was submitted by the society to the Polite Arts Committee, who invited opinions from Paul Sandby, Thomas Malton, John Downman, and a lesser known artist named Sherwin.

No sooner had Sandby and Malton, and incidentally also Robert Adam, given their opinions than the Society was approached by William Reeves, who had learned of his brother's action. He claimed that the 'British ink' submitted was as much his invention as his brother's, and that Thomas had stolen a march on him at a time when he had been more than usually preoccupied with the production of a set of new stamps for the marking of the firm's colour-cakes. Given a week, he said, he would send them a sample of his own making which would be (sic) 'superior to any yett exhibited, and if you should be so obliged to defer that ink till mine can be adgudge and give bounty to them that deserves the best'.

William's sample was duly sent to the same artists as had received Thomas's, and it was decided that a final opinion should be given jointly on the two samples. Not all the recipients bothered to report. Malton's reaction was tepid; he said that it did not effect a dark enough stain on the paper. Paul Sandby, to satisfy himself that Thomas's sample was

[23]

actually produced by Thomas, made a journey of inspection to Holborn Bridge, but we know nothing of his verdict on the quality of the ink. A certain Hincks, a miniaturist, was enthusiastic. Robert Adam, in a letter dated April 21st, 1784, wrote that he had 'made constant use' of Mr. Reeves ink. Malton seems to have agreed with Hincks, while another artist, William Green, declared the ink to be superior to anything of its kind made in England. The Polite Arts Committee added a rider to the effect that the ink appeared to 'wash up' more easily than China ink, but that this defect could easily be rectified by the makers.

There the matter ended; the brothers' open dissension had clearly embarrassed the Society of Arts and had probably influenced them against making any kind of award. What commercial advantage accrued to one or other, or both brothers, henceforward competitors, from the introduction of the new ink we do not know. But it doubtless enhanced the prestige of the name of Reeves that so notable a figure as Robert Adam had confessed to making habitual use of it, and it seems more than likely that others of his profession followed suit.

In 1785, William was elected a member of the Society of Arts, who consulted him from time to time as new colour samples were submitted to them; but thereafter we lose sight of him. The future was to belong to Thomas and his descendants, for whom affairs were now to take a peculiarly profitable turn.

It is probable that Reeves were already suppliers to Christ's Hospital and to a number of other schools. It is almost certain that they supplied several of the leading Military Academies. The drawing masters at these academies were frequently painters of some repute and men of influence in the world of art. Turner's great friend, William Frederick Wells, prime mover in the formation of the Society of Painters in Water-Colours, was for thirty years Professor of Drawing at

A Wayside Inn (Duke of Cumberland Inn, Woolwich Common). Paul Sandby (Water-colour tint with pen outlines. c. 1772).

Durham Cathedral. Thomas Hearne (Water-colour. 1783)

Addiscombe Military Academy; William Sawrey Gilpin, the animal painter and the first president of the Society, was Drawing Master at the Royal Military College at Great Marlow, and later at Sandhurst; William Delamotte, pupil of Benjamin West, was also at Great Marlow; Andrew Wilson, the landscape painter, was like Gilpin at Sandhurst.

Significantly, Addiscombe was the training ground for regiments maintained in India by the East India Company. Reeves would seem already to have had a brushing acquaintance with the Company, for an analysis of their 'British ink' showed it to be an imitation of the 'stick ink' used by artists and draughtsmen in China, samples of which could only have been imported into England for their examination through the Company, who exercised a monopoly in such matters. Their fortunes were soon to be more closely linked.

The foundation of Reeves business in India, which was to flourish for some seventy years, was private custom; contractual supplies to the East India Company were, however, to follow. By the last two decades of the eighteenth century the resident English community in India was large and prosperous; especially was this so in Calcutta. Life had acquired a settled pattern; English culture had been firmly implanted. For many there was abundant leisure, giving rise to a new curiosity, and wonderment at the luxuriance of the Indian landscape and the beauty of the native architecture, which translated itself into a natural desire to record as much as could be seen.

Reference to issues of the *Calcutta Gazette* for the years 1784, –5, and –6, shows that, besides pictures, artists' materials were being regularly shipped to India. The vogue for amateur water-colour painting and sketching was expanding rapidly. Professional landscape and portrait painters, too, quick to see their opportunities, were sailing for India, where they were picking up substantial private commissions from English merchants and officials, as well as from prominent Indians; some even settled there permanently. Among the earliest arrivals were Tilly Kettle, the portrait painter, George Willison, and William Hodges, the official artist on Captain Cook's Pacific voyage.

Johann Zoffany arrived in the autumn of 1783, remaining for six years. His first commission was for a portrait of Sir Elijah Impey, Chief Justice of the Supreme Court, intended as a tribute from the Calcutta Bar. There can be little doubt that Zoffany prospered, but a press report in 1785 must surely have exaggerated his earnings: 'The emigration of artists has received an additional spur by Zoffany's having already remitted home £36,000, accompanied with a letter which states that he intends coming home as soon as he has finished the portraits that are bespoke, which will produce to the amount of £30,000 more.'

Ozias Humphrey, never one to lag behind, promptly took the hint and sailed for India, where he executed a number of portraits and several water-colours. His example was followed with profit by Charles Smith and by Arthur William Davis, who spent about ten years in India. In 1784, Thomas Daniell arrived with his nephew William; he, too, stayed for ten years and, with William's help, completed on his return a large work called *Oriental Scenery*, the drawings for which were later exhibited at the Walker Galleries in Bond Street.

The demand for materials created by the passage of so many artists, and by the impetus their presence in India gave to the swelling ranks of amateur practitioners, brought Reeves a welcome expansion of trade. A curiously interesting, though tragic incident bears witness to one of their earlier shipments. On January 6th, 1786, the East Indiaman *Halsewell* (the ship in which George Willison had returned to England five years before, and in which Zoffany had sailed to India two years later) was wrecked, when outward bound, with heavy loss of life off the Dorset coast. Among the dead was her master, Captain Pierce.

Pierce was a man of some cultivation, and kept on board a band of musicians; a print of the time shows a music party in progress at the windows of the *Halsewell's* stern cabins. Reporting the disaster, the *Morning Chronicle* wrote of Pierce that he had had 'a great taste for the polite arts', and had been particularly helpful to Zoffany in recommending him to likely patrons on his arrival in India. The report then proceeds to a reference that among the missing effects was 'a large assortment of curious boxes of superfine colours, crayons, black lead pencils, with a great variety of articles for drawing, manufactured by Messrs. Reeves and Son, Holborn Bridge'. (From the addition of 'and Son' it is also to be concluded that by this time Thomas's son, William, had joined him in the business.)

Two other items are relevant to this period. In an advertisement of 1788, Thomas Reeves informs merchants and ships' captains in the East and West India trades that they can be supplied at Messrs. Champante and Whitrow, Jewry Street, Aldgate, conveniently adjacent to the river. In an issue of *The Times* for November 7th, 1805, Reeves and Co., in an advertisement, cautioned 'Captains, Pursers, and others trading to India' against the activities of an East-end trader who had been selling a counterfeit version of Reeves colour cakes, which he claimed to be the genuine article and on which he had had stamped the Reeves name and trade mark.

Thomas Reeves was not, himself, to enjoy the fruits of the East India Company trade, which fell to his son after his death. But all the pioneer work had been his; without the aid of the private trade which he had built up over the years, the Company's business would never have been secured. Other awards and satisfactions, however, were yet to come his way. He became supplier to the Royal Family, and to 'their Drawing Academy, Military and Naval'. In addition to colours, he was selling 'every article for drawing miniatures, landscapes, portraits, mapping, signals, fortifications, etc.' His stock in trade included Italian and English crayons, pencils, ink, palettes, knives, drawing paper, and articles for use with oil and water-colours.

The business had been established on a sound footing and the future prospects for his son looked more than promising. In 1790, the firm received the grant of Royal Warrants from Queen Charlotte and from the Prince of Wales, afterwards George IV. Six years later, to his immense personal satisfaction, the worthy Thomas was elected President of the Amicable Society of Old Blues, a select society associated with his old school, at a meeting of which he had come upon the poet Coleridge when the latter was still a senior scholar of Christ's Hospital. In the summer of 1799, he died at his home in Tottenham at the age of sixty-three.

Thomas's son, William, appears to have applied himself to the business with all the energy and acumen his father would have desired. Despite the existence, by now, of such competitors as Rowneys, Blackman and Newman (the two last-named being, respectively, the firms of George Blackman, son-in-law of William the elder, and that of James Newman, Blackman's erstwhile pupil), young Reeves, with William Woodyer, whom he had taken into partnership, continued to prosper. Several fine trade cards survive from the first half of the nineteenth century, some pasted inside the lids of colour boxes. One of these, dating from the time when the firm was Reeves and Woodyer, besides bearing the company's arms, along with the Royal Arms and the Prince of Wales feathers, carries the additional inscription: 'colour-makers to the Honourable East India Company'. An investigation of the massive volumes of the East India Company's financial and trading archives has revealed a few of the details of Reeves trade with the Company, or 'John Company' as it has been termed.

Isaac Smith's paint box

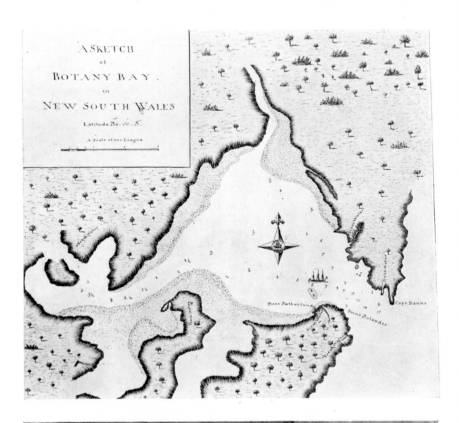

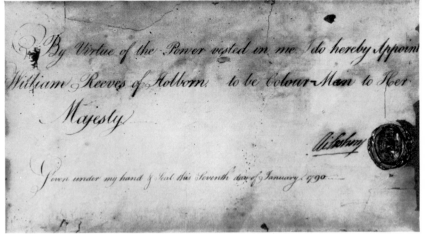

Botany Bay. Isaac Smith (Sketch. c. 1770)
The Royal Warrant awarded to Reeves, 1790

The goods sold included stationery as well as colour boxes, although the firm of William Balston appears to have supplied most of the paper. The colour boxes were intended for use by officers on survey duties in India; they were also distributed for training purposes and as prizes at Addiscombe. An entry for £76 is shown for these items, covering the period of the last four months of 1819. It is a reasonable assumption that the company's civil service college at Haileybury was also a customer at this time. Historically interesting is a modest order for hair pencils from Sir Hudson Lowe, Governor of St. Helena, for 'the residence of General Buonoparte'. In 1820 and 1821, a large number of colour boxes were shipped out to India as Military Stores, and in response to demands from the Company's 'Territorial and Political' Department.

Entries in the Company's General Cash Journal for 1830 show that the pattern of demand was still largely composed of military and civil branches, and the training establishment at Addiscombe, and that the size of this demand had, over the years, steadily multiplied. Without digging any deeper into the details of transactions, it is evident that the Company's orders, coupled with the continuing private trade in India, still contributed handsomely to Reeves income. William John Reeves, when he died in 1827, was a man of substance much respected in the City, where he held the office of deputy to the Alderman of Holborn.

The business now devolved on James and Henry, 'W.J.'s' sons. Challenging times lay ahead for both men, more particularly for Henry whose contribution was to prove more solid and lasting than his brother's. The Industrial Revolution was the signal for a prodigious explosion of human energy which was to last until the end of the nineteenth century. Of this period a distinguished historian has written, 'Without being conscious of what he was about, Man, by means of his newly invented machines, was changing the conditions of his life with a rapidity which would have constituted an inevitable death sentence on any other animal'. For Reeves the tempo and competitive element in trade and manufacture was to grow steadily more ferocious, calling for all the industry and ingenuity they were able to supply.

In 1832, Winsor and Newton was founded. Newton was a chemist who applied his scientific knowledge to the choice of colours with considerable skill; William Winsor was an artist with a wide acquaintance in the art world. Their association was to constitute a rivalry to the firm of Reeves, more enduring and powerful than any other. Reeves initial response to the challenge found expression in technical innovations and in a modest measure of diversification into a range of stationery products. Later in the century, after the Indian Mutiny had brought about a collapse in their thriving trade in India, they were to reassert their supremacy in the educational market.

With the passage of the English School, the requirements of the artist had grown more sophisticated. Until the emergence of the 'artist's colourman' the labour of self-preparation, not only of colours but of canvasses and all the other requisites of an artist, had necessitated the operation of a system of hired workshop assistants. This system disappeared when supplies of equipment and ready made colours became available. Parallel with this 'technological' change the artist shed his medieval inheritance and acquired a new social status. The Romantic movement of the early nineteenth century radically revised the conception of the painter from that of a quasi-craftsman serving a specific purpose or meeting the wishes of a particular patron to that of an artist in his own right exercising his talents solely as a means of expression. The abandonment of the workshop system and, with it, the almost exclusive practise of studio working as artists resorted more and more to outside locations, introduced a weight of dependence upon the colourmen heavier than they could at first bear.

But it was clear to people like Reeves that, implicit in the challenge lay more than practical commercial advantage; they alone, by the applied results of their scientific investigations, could improve, cheapen, and widen the range of artists' materials, and so give a unique impetus to English painting at a time when a great evolutionary stage in its progress was about to begin. The transition is underlined by the wholly different character of the recipes and instructions used by painters.

By the eighteenth century the emphasis on the handling of raw materials had begun to be displaced by discussions of processes and methods; by the nineteenth century manufactured materials had come to be taken for granted, the main concern being the provision of information to the painter on such matters as use and effect, scientific analyses of materials and methods affecting reliability and permanence, light phenomena, etc. The age of specialisation was firmly taking root. The painter's task, from now on, was to seek a market for his pictures; the colourmen's to supply him with all his materials ready for use. As the market grew, so the painter applied himself to his art with increasing dexterity. In the process his requirements became more critical, his need for assurance on the point of behaviour of the colours he bought more exacting.

It would be false to suggest that the early technical advances of the colourmen meant an end to improvisation. The instincts of the craftsman died hard; the idiosyncratic flights of the creative artist were not to be grounded by science. What the colourmen did at this stage was to extend the facilities for improvisation, and to make ampler provision for the lesser skills.

Turner was perhaps the greatest master of manipulation, fertile in such expedients as the abrading and rubbing away of the surface of the paper to prepare for the greater delineation of form, even cutting off a layer of the paper with a knife to take out a high light. William Hunt, the rustic figure- and still-life painter, would sometimes plough up the paper with a knife to give added contrast between flesh and garment. George Barrett used bread to erase high lights; Gilpin treated his lights with an initial coating of spirit varnish which, after he had applied water-colour to the surface in the normal way, he removed with spirits of wine. John Varley, late in life, adopted a plan which consisted of straining a sheet of common whitey-brown paper over ordinary drawing paper; on the former he painted the subject in rich tints and for the high lights he rubbed away the coarse paper down to the pure white surface beneath. Cotman sometimes mixed his pigments with sour paste. Copley Fielding constantly impressed upon his students the merit of the manipulative processes. But such resorts were not for the less accomplished, and certainly not for the amateur who was to account for an increasing proportion of the colourman's sales.

From the succession of James and Henry Reeves, and throughout the nineteenth century, technical advances were governed by competition, but also by two new factors: air pollution caused by concentrations of industry, and the expansion of world trade. Many new pigments were discovered but some of these, for example the anilines, proved wholly unsuitable for the professional artist's use. With the growth of towns and cities appreciable quantities of sulphur and other destructive gases entered the atmosphere, causing more harm to pigments than is generally realised even today.

A number of organic pigments were imported, including cochineal crimson, prepared from the dried body of the female insect of that name. Although used by Spanish artists in the sixteenth century, this was really a very fugitive pigment suitable only for colouring foodstuffs. Another organic pigment was Indian yellow, prepared from the urine of cows fed on mango leaves. When cleaned and powdered, this

The Villa d'Este. J. R. Cozens (Water-colour. c. 1780–90)

Kirkstall Abbey. Thomas Girtin (Water-colour. c. 1801)

emerged as a beautiful golden yellow glazing colour, and it was quite permanent. Eventually, however, the Indian government forbade its production on the ground of cruelty to the cows; a later substitute was formed with coal-tar pigments such as naptha yellow. Gamboge, a vegetable gum proof against acid, was also imported at this time and is still in use, as were buckthorn for the manufacture of sap green, Persian berries for yellow lake, and indigo, a relation of woad, which had been used by the ancient Britons. Some of these imports were doubtless paid for on a *quid pro quo* basis, set against the rising export trade in artists' materials.

At home the chemists were busy producing inorganic pigments from the by-products of new industrial processes. Many of these were non-resistant to air pollution and were later discarded by the reputable colourmen. The bulk of the permanent pigments, however, owe their discovery to this period, the cobalt and cerulean blues, for instance, the first a clear-toned pigment, the latter a wholly durable colour; the yellow and orange cadmiums, useful in all techniques with the possible exception of fresco; the alizarin crimsons, one of the coal-tar group, composed chiefly of carbon, hydrogen, and nitrogen, with the frequent addition of sulphur; and that beautiful and permanent green viridian, the brilliant transparency of which the old masters would have rightly coveted.

Concurrent with the introduction of new colours, considerable advances were made in the provision of suitable paper through successive stages of dissatisfaction with the earlier wire-laid, common white cartridge, and hand-made vellum. Ruskin in one of his Manchester lectures went so far as to advocate that the Government should undertake the manufacture of a perfectly pure paper made from linen rags of the highest possible quality, and should stamp each sheet so made. But to treat of the paper-makers would enlarge the scope of this essay too much.

[33]

Mention is made by Gilbert Redgrave, in his *Water-Colour Painting in England*, of Winsor and Newton's employment of metal tubes 'for the moist colours, similar to those used for oil paints'. There is some lack of confirmation on this point. The original patent covering collapsible tin tubes for use with oil colours appears to have been taken out in America in 1841, by a certain Mr. John Rand. There is evidence, however, that they were invented several years prior to this date. Certainly they were in general use in this country by 1845, probably manufactured by a process of extrusion for which Rand had taken out a further patent in 1842. From 1862 onwards Reeves were supplied with these tubes from the still active firm of Sanders. Whatever their actual source or original point of sale, the tube proved to be of lasting satisfaction and a welcome substitute for the old bladder bags.

Reeves trade in hand-made pencils was regarded at this time to be important enough for the firm to publish advertisements warning the public against imitations. Of far greater importance, however, was their experimental work, begun in 1844, on the employment of virgin wax as a water-colour paint medium in place of gum. This work met with instant success, and glowing testimonials were received from many leading painters, among whom were Henry Warren, President of the National Society of Painters in Water-Colour, William Hunt, Clarkson Stanfield, Copley Fielding, and Hablot Browne, who won fame as the illustrator of Dickens's early works.

In the Spring of 1849, Reeves sent a box of the new wax colours to the Royal Society of Arts, pointing out that since their last submission, in 1781, great improvements had been made in the manufacture and preparation of colours, 'but none equal to that we have made within the last few years in the preparation of our cake colours by the Introduction of wax as a medium in lieu of gum, and which has given such universal satisfaction amongst the eminent artists of the present day'. They added that they had also made some wax colours in a form convenient for use in architects' and engineers' drawing offices, and submitted samples of these.

Two years later, the year of the Great Exhibition, Reeves received a medal for their moist colours, which they marketed in gutta percha pans, and a glowing notice in the *Illustrated London News*, commending them on their whole range of colours and hand-made pencils. Of their wax colours the author wrote that they possessed 'great volume and transparency', approximating to the character of oil paints, and maintained their softness excellently in hot climates. These two qualities were of the greatest significance.

Capitalising on their successful experience in India, Reeves were now extending their overseas trade rapidly. Records reveal sales at this time to Peru, Brazil, Russia and the United States; the first two countries obviously set no little score on the ability of imported colours to stand up to the rigours of their climate. At the same time, or to be precise rather earlier, a methodological change, originally inspired by Paul Sandby was swiftly gaining ground among the professional artists aimed at imparting more 'substance' to their water-colours. The motive behind this change was an increasingly widespread dissatisfaction with the showing of water-colours at public exhibitions; they had enjoyed a somewhat Cinderella-like status, being either consigned to the basement or placed in the most disadvantageous juxtaposition to oil paintings. Many painters sought a partial remedy for this gross disparity in apparent substance between oil and water-colour by the re-employment of white, or body-colour. To them the new wax water-colours 'approximating in character to oil paints' must have been a singular boon.

Reeves had already moved their premises from Holborn to Cheapside, an address convenient to the City where they enjoyed a flourishing stationery trade. This was in 1829. In

1831, they opened a branch in Throgmorton Street. Sixteen years later James Reeves retired from the business and went to live at Danemore Park, near Tonbridge, where he died in 1868. His younger brother, Henry, took into partnership his sister's child, Henry Bowles Wild, of whom the present chairman of the company is a descendant; and in the same year Charles Kemp Wild, another nephew, joined the firm at the age of sixteen. When Henry Reeves died in 1877, eleven years after his retirement, a bachelor like his brother, control of the firm passed to the Wilds.

One of the first decisions to be made by Henry and Charles Wild—a decision of considerable importance as reflecting not only the substantial volume of their current business, but also the measure of their future expectations—was to remove from Cheapside and to establish the firm on a very much larger site they had acquired in Dalston. Previously all manufacture had taken place at Cheapside, the grinding and mixing of the colours being performed in a temporary workshop built on the roof. Even so, there was too little space, and the colour drying pans had to be fitted up in a top room of the next door house. Moreover, not only had it become increasingly difficult to run the business efficiently in such cramped quarters but there was an ever-present risk of causing an offence against the local bye-laws by carrying on an industrial operation in what was an acknowledged sanctum of commerce.

Dalston, then a purely residential district, lay four miles to the north of the City and was served by the first of the suburban lines, the North London Railway. The Wilds bought the plot from the railway for the modest sum of £750 and, at an additional cost of £3,200, built their factory of four floors and a basement. Here the firm of Reeves were to be established for the next seventy years, making further extensions from time to time as required. Steam-driven machinery for the grinding of colours, which could never have been accommodated at

[36]

W.^m & T. REEVES,
Superfine Colour Makers,
At the Blue Coat Boy, N.º 2 Well Yard,
Little Brittain, LONDON:
Prepares all sorts of Fine Colours to the greatest
Perfection: Double & Single Setts of Crayons, in
all the Different Shades equal to the Italian, Colours
for Minature Painting. Compleat setts of Colours in
Potts, all arranged to Work at a touch, in any Climate:
and free from Cracking, fine Colours for Painting on silks.
Setts of Colours in Phials, for Planning & Mapping.
Boxes of Drops, Shells, & fine Colours Ground in Spirits,
& Oil. LIKEWISE Their new Invented Cakes of
all Colours, which will Work equal to the finest India.
Ink. Fine Camp Paper, Black, Blue, and Red, for
taking of Drawings. Transparent Paper for Tracing:
Fine India Ink, and all Articles for Drawing.

WHOLESALE & RETAIL & FOR EXPORTATION.

N.B. Pictures Carefully Cleand, Lind & Repaird.

Early Reeves Trade Card. c. 1770

The Greater Silver Palette awarded to Reeves, 1781

Cheapside, was now introduced, earning the factory the quaint name of 'Reeves Steam Colour Works'. The Cheapside building was retained as a sales outlet and as the administrative headquarters of the firm.

The move to Dalston coincided approximately with the highly important shift in emphasis in the direction of the educational market already briefly mentioned. In the fifties Reeves had begun to publish on their own account a number of books intended to be of practical use to amateur and professional artists. In 1852, appeared the *Amateur Artists' Companion*, containing a guide to oil-colour painting, biographies of well-known living artists, and a variety of informative items of the kind that were later published annually in Reeves *The Year's Arts*. In the 1853 edition 'A Short History of Painting' was included among the contents. With the publication of a *Manual of the First Principles of Drawing*, by C. H. Weigall, Reeves interest in art education had become clearly marked.

Some attention had already been paid to this market, which had supplied Reeves with a steady, if insubstantial, proportion of their income. In addition to sales of materials to the military academies, and to such foundation schools as Christ's Hospital, there were the requirements to be met of a host of private academies for the education of the sons and daughters of the upper and middle classes, most of whom boasted drawing masters and at which, more particularly at the young ladies' establishments, an ability to draw and sketch was an essential 'accomplishment'. But the 'mass' market was yet to be established.

By 1850, art had been included in the curriculum of such State-aided teaching centres as the National and British Schools, represented in towns and villages all over the country; while the spirit of the 1851 Exhibition had acted as a signal spur to the wider dissemination of knowledge and appreciation of the principles of art and design. It was not, however,

[37]

until the Elementary Education Act of 1870 that the teaching of art in the free schools approached anything like general practise. The expansion of Reeves opportunities really, therefore, started in the period following this Act. It was well that it did, for with the Indian Mutiny of 1857 the career of the East India Company hastened to its end.

In the closing stages Reeves annual turnover with the Company had been in the region of £6,000, or between 25 per cent and 30 per cent of the firm's total turnover. So high a proportion of sales would require a formidable effort to replace. It may also be assumed that in the development of the East India custom a part at least of Reeves manufacturing must have been geared to the production of items not likely to be in general demand—such untoward exports as, for instance drawing papers in rolls fifty-four inches wide, cakes of colour four times the standard size, to say nothing of a consignment of haversacks made of American cloth and having three divisions, one to hold a field book, one for a pint bottle, and one for the reception of biscuits and cheese. But the brothers Wild lacked neither industry nor resource, and were not to be deterred by the challenge. The Science and Art Department at South Kensington was soon persuaded to become a regular and substantial customer; the War Office extended their custom and, not to be despised since it could well have set the trend for others, the Ordnance Survey Office at Southampton placed an order with Reeves for a quantity of Persian blue in powder form.

The Elementary Education Act of 1870 did not immediately result in comprehensive compulsory education, but it did have the effect of extending systematic teaching to a far wider number of children than had ever received it before. Also, art had become a part of the curriculum. The approach to the subject was exceedingly literal and unimaginative, having perhaps a closer affinity to design than to creative

[38]

art. Nonetheless, it was more than a beginning and inherent in it was the promise of a very real harvest for Reeves.

Modestly at first, but with growing impetus the firm's educational sales grew. In 1875, they were suppliers to the London School Board. By the turn of the century they were sufficiently well established to reap the major benefit from the welter of current ideas which were effectively transforming the whole conceptual approach to the teaching of art in the schools. An increasing number of teachers were concerned to widen the process beyond that of pencilled line work and copyist 'drawing lessons' to the point of admission of the children's expression of their individual ideas and personalities.

A pioneer of this enlightened movement was Joseph Vaughan, formerly an art teacher with the London School Board, at this time Art Organiser for Glasgow, then acknowledged to be the most advanced of all cities in artistic achievement and appreciation. Charles James Wild, son of C. K. Wild, who had since succeeded to the chairmanship of Reeves (by now a public company), which office he was to occupy with brilliant success for a quarter of a century, had the good fortune to meet Vaughan. Infected by Vaughan's enthusiasm and clear vision of the future, Wild, who had long harboured the view that Reeves brightest prospect in the educational market lay in the growth of brush work in the schools' art classes, seized the advantages offered by the new movement with both hands.

At his instigation, Reeves had during the previous decade branched out into the ownership of a number of retail shops, one at St. John's Wood, two in Kensington, one in Charing Cross Road, one in Moorgate; the firm had also gained control of the old established business of Lechertier Barbe with the intention of using it as a departure point for the opening of further retail shops out of London, of which Brighton was to be the first choice. The idea of establishing oneself in locations

[39]

convenient to one's potential customers, and especially in quarters where colonies of professional artists were known to reside, seemed logical in the extreme. In practice, however, it turned out to be the least profitable of all Wild's enterprises, the out-of-London shops being a near calamity. But it had taught him a bitter lesson in the differentials of selling techniques. When it came to the education market he was quick to realise that the sort of travellers whose training stood them in admirable stead when dealing with shops which sold Reeves goods were considerably less effective in interpreting the needs and satisfying the demands of local authorities.

Joseph Vaughan had made great play of the basic requirement for a representative who could devote his whole time to meeting art teachers up and down the country, and to a close study of their needs; he even suggested the man for the job, a Mr. George Mason, then a teacher with the London School Board. Mason was appointed as Reeves Educational Adviser, and took up his post in 1904. He appears to have been a pleasant, genial man, with a wide experience in his profession, and he was to prove an outstanding success.

What colour work was done in the art classes of schools at this time was mainly done with wax crayons; water-colours were in some instances employed but their application was confined largely to the execution of blobs and geometrical patterns. A more catholic approach was advocated by Vaughan, with the support of a number of progressive-minded art inspectors and organisers, notably in Leeds and Birmingham but elsewhere besides. It swiftly won the approval of the Chief Education Officers in most of the major towns and in the populous counties of the south-east, while the National Union of Teachers extended it every encouragement.

The effect was to widen the range, and to increase the scale of purchases from the schools themselves and from the Supplies

Officers of the Education Authorities, and to accelerate the demands from consumers for the expert counsel of George Mason. Reeves introduced their water-colour boxes and brushes into the elementary schools, and a greater variety of pencils, crayons and stumping chalks. Within a year of Mason's appointment they were receiving their first orders from the London County Council, which had now absorbed the activities of the London School Board. To meet increased orders for brushes arising from the spread of free brush work in the art classes a new building was erected on an adjoining site at Dalston; here hog brushes were also made, for the oil colour trade. By 1907 Reeves trade in brushes was regarded as important enough for George Mason to consider it worth his while to write a book on brush work techniques for sole distribution to Scottish art teachers.

Reference to Reeves catalogues in the first years of the present century reveal few changes in the range of their products. Colour boxes and brushes followed a standard pattern, while supplies of chalks and pastels had still to be imported from France. The changes wrought were in the volume of sales, which show a steady expansion. In 1909, however, when increasingly pastel work was either displacing or being used in combination with pencil work, and when dissatisfaction was growing with wax crayons, which could neither be blended nor merged, Reeves introduced for the first time a series of pastels of their own make. This pioneer enterprise developed into the famous 'Greyhound' pastel, which appeared in 1911; modestly priced, it scored an immediate success. Again the Dalston works had to be enlarged to accommodate stocks of this new product; to finance the new development the firm's nominal capital was raised from £100,000 to £150,000.

George Mason, whose advice was by now being regularly sought by education authorities in the drafting of contracts for the supply of art materials to the primary schools, was obliged to take on two assistants, one to cover Scotland and the North, the other to travel the South. In 1910, he was sent on a 'British Manufacturers' tour of Canada, where he laid the foundation of Reeves large and expanding trade in that country. A year later his son joined him in the business, remaining for close on fifty years. Meanwhile another family connection had joined the board of Reeves, Louis Charles Simmons, whose mother was a daughter of C. K. Wild.

The First World War brought an inevitable setback to Reeves fortunes, which during C. J. Wild's direction had more than doubled despite further costly additions to the Dalston works. A number of retail branches, by 1917 nearly all those in the City, had to be closed down. With many directors and senior executives away in the forces, a heavy burden fell on C. J. Wild, who virtually made his home in the factory, working frequently far into the night. The Russian Revolution of 1917 dealt another blow, debts from Russian customers to the tune of nearly £5,000 having to be written off from the profits of that year. Following the Armistice, three members of the Simmons family returned to the firm, two joining the board. In 1920, George Mason died suddenly, and the reins of his office passed to his son, G. H. L. Mason.

Swift expansion followed the war. In 1922 a new product was evolved, the terrachrome crayon which, having a china clay base and no wax content, proved harder than pastel and almost proof against powdering. Between 1919 and 1922, the company's sales were almost doubled, and a move from Dalston was rendered imperative. In 1921, eleven acres of land were purchased at Enfield, where the Greyhound works still occupied by Reeves gradually took shape. In 1923, Charles James Wild died, and in the following year Reginald Herbert Harrison, now vice-chairman and managing director, related to the Wilds on his mother's side, joined the firm.

Besides catering for the needs of professional and amateur artists, of institutions and government departments at home and overseas, of schools and academies, of the exponents of the ubiquitous cartoons and advertisement designs of the Victorian era, Reeves were to derive new and substantial benefits from yet another phenomenon of British pictorial art—the poster. Particularly after the 1914-18 war, the poster artist made far more use than ever before of bright, striking colours, while the advance in advertising techniques was accompanied by a fast growing requirement for liquid Indian ink and coloured lithograph work. To meet these needs, which were soon duplicated by the schools, Reeves stepped up their production of powdered poster colours, the sales of which reached a sufficient volume to justify the addition, in 1927, of two extra bays to the Enfield factory for the accommodation of new plant for the striking and mixing of colours.

The same year saw a marked increase in the company's pigment-making capacity, and the inauguration of Reeves and Sons (Canada) Ltd., which was to develop into one of their most important overseas subsidiaries. Interesting merely as an echo from the past, the artists' colourmen James Newman Ltd., a business which had survived from its establishment by the Newman who was a pupil of the original William Reeves a century and a half earlier, offered itself for sale to Reeves and Sons. The offer was not immediately accepted, but negotiations were re-opened in 1936, when a sale was successfully concluded.

By the 1930s the pace of competition had rendered even greater the need to keep abreast, better still in advance of current innovations and practises. Reeves added to their staff a research chemist, a Dr. L. J. Dunn. At the British Industries Fair of 1933 Winsor and Newton's exhibits included for the first time a range of materials specifically designed for the

[43]

educational trade. These materials were closely modelled on Reeves products.

It fell to Mr. B. D. Wild, the present chairman, to formulate a response to this very serious competitive challenge. A new drive was instituted, aimed at professional artists and art school students. Advertisements were placed in art periodicals, a retaining fee was paid to the artist Lawrence East for his advice, and every new advantage was sought from the latest developments in the field of educational colour-work. The most notable of these had arisen from the experiments of Professor W. Ostwald, the eminent chemist. Ostwald introduced a new colour range, still used by some teachers, which was based on the spectrum, each spectral tint being distinguished in juxtaposition with its opposite tint. Reeves put on the market the range of colours required by the Ostwald system with an explanatory book. After two years Reeves produced a new range of colours, the composition and consistency of which exceeded in degree those which had been designed to supplement the Ostwald system.

Meanwhile the forces of modern psychological thought processes were beginning to impinge on the theory of art teaching in schools. Important work had already been carried out in Vienna by a Professor Cisek. This work, which was directed towards the encouragement of freer play for children's self-expressive urges, had its counterpart in the movement devoted to the same principles which was being so vigorously conducted in England in London and elsewhere, by Mr. R. R. Tomlinson, Principal of the Central School of Arts and Crafts and, for twenty-five years, Senior Inspector of Art Education to the London County Council; also by Miss Marion Richardson, who performed notable work in this field.

Basic to the new theory of teaching was an insistence that children should be encouraged to draw more freely, with the full sweep of the arm as we are told was the habit of the

[44]

Europe a Prophecy. William Blake (Water-colour; book illustration. 1794)

In a Shoreham Garden. Samuel Palmer (Water-colour, gouache. c. 1829)

earliest cave artists of Altamira and Lascaux. This could only be done, however, if the children were supplied with larger sheets of paper. A predicament also arose over paint; the small amounts contained in the cakes of a box of water-colours were soon exhausted by this new practice. Clearly, a new device was needed, more akin to poster colours. But first came a period of trial and experimentation, with resort to expediencies not unreminiscent of Paul Sandby's ingenious play with the 'bye-product' of burnt toast. Marion Richardson recalls how, before the colourmen finally 'came up with' the solution, her pupils resorted to the improvised use of such constituents as curry powder, beetroot juice, and gravy browning.*

The answer when it came was in the development of powder colours, containing their own fixative and housed in large glass jars suitable for storage on classroom shelves. The first to manufacture these powder colours were Reeves, who also pioneered their massive development. This was in 1935; by 1938, they were producing them on a really large scale. At the same time they brought out a range of liquid tempera colours, a cheaper version of their poster and showcard colours, and a new series of high-class crayons containing a small proportion of wax. The familiar tins of tempera paste followed after the war.

An activity peripheral to their trade in artists' materials was carried on by Reeves between the two wars which, while not strictly relevant to our theme, deserves mention for the commercial advantage it brought and for the technical skills within the company which made it possible. In 1927 Reeves had set up at Enfield a new colour striking plant for fast pigments. From this plant the company established for itself a big name in the trade as suppliers of permanent pigments to a variety of industries. The wallpaper manufacturers were

*Marion Richardson, *Art and the Child*, University of London Press, 1948, p. 48.

their customers from the outset, with their requirements for permanent water-colours for the hand-painting of friezes, and sometimes for whole wall designs. Reeves pigments were used for the printing of postage stamps, particularly red ones. Messrs. de la Rue bought colours for the printing of bank notes, while yellows were supplied to Messrs. Waterlow for a similar purpose and with a special reference to Portugal. For some years before the Second World War Reeves were the only suppliers of madders and madder lakes, colours of particular importance. They supplied pigments to the motor industry where they were used in the finishes applied to car bodies, especially maroon, a colour much in vogue at one time. In addition to these and other sources of industrial sales, they enjoyed the custom of a number of printing ink manufacturers, among them Ault and Wiborg.

The cumulative effect of Reeves researches and consequent improvement in the quality of their colours, which had brought them so much success in the educational, industrial, and professional and amateur water-colour fields, finally determined the board to review their existing range of oil colours. The Artists' Oil Colours which had long borne their name were withdrawn, and new colours were substituted. These borrowed their name from the famous Spanish painter, Francisco Goya; they were called Goya colours. A competition was organised for artists using these colours, and in the spring of 1936 the New Burlington Gallery in London was rented for an exhibition of the successful entries. Thereafter Goya colours entered, as it were, into the vocabulary of many leading painters' requirements. When, two years later, the French Government sponsored an exhibition of Goya's paintings in Paris, two of Reeves directors took a party of students from London art schools to France. Later in the same year this enlightened policy of promotion took the form of a summer sketching school in Brittany. In 1939, a similar trip was made to Normandy.

The Second World War brought Reeves an ample share of the common disasters, of bombing and tragic loss of life. The pattern of their products remained substantially unchanged, with the grim exception of the manufacture of anti-gas ointment. At a time of extra difficulty their old competitors, Winsor and Newton, voluntarily lent a hand with the production of students' materials so that they could meet outstanding school contracts. Fortunately arrangements were already in force with Messrs. James Bell of Melbourne for the making of Greyhound pastels.

The early years of the war were particularly hard and brought the familiar train of financial loss and resultant scrimping, but by 1942, with the cessation of air raids, a remarkable recovery was made, sales rising by over £50,000. Artists' brushes were a valuable wartime export, and Reeves joined the Brush Export Group of the British Brush Manufacturers' Association. For the remainder of hostilities business continued to expand.

By 1948 Reeves were actively renewing their overseas contacts and establishing new ones. Their managing director visited Canada and the United States; selling agents were appointed for the first time in New York, Chicago and Los Angeles. A further visit followed in 1951; the new Canadian office and warehouse at Toronto were inspected, customers were called upon as far west as British Columbia. In the same year the United Nations Educational, Scientific, and Cultural Organisation held an international seminar on art education at the University of Bristol, at which Reeves exhibited their materials. An international Society for Education through Art was formed; Mr. Mason attended their assemblies, making a host of valuable international connections.

In 1958, larger premises had to be taken for Reeves Canadian subsidiary company, today Canada's largest supplier of art materials, and to give better service to customers in the west a warehouse had later to be opened in Vancouver. In 1959 an American associate company was formed, Reeves and Sons Inc. During the previous decade Reeves sales in America had been promoted by their agents located in all the principle areas; the new company instituted an intensive programme of market research before the formulation and execution from 1961 of a systematic, nation-wide sales policy. To secure a foothold in Latin America a Mexican subsidiary was acquired, the business of which was the production and sales of carbon papers, stamp pads, typewriter ribbons, and other similar items. Reeves have an Australian subsidiary in Melbourne, and an associated company in Bombay. In 1964 came a further acquisition: a controlling interest in South African Leather Colourers and Dyers Ltd., since renamed Reeves (South Africa) (Pty.) Ltd., manufacturers of special purpose dyes, stains, and cleaners for leather and plastic goods.

This year, 1966, finds Reeves and Sons in the pride of their bi-centenary. Among the currently established artists' colour-men the distinction of having traded continuously for two hundred years is unique. But the burden imposed on the management's skill, technical efficiency, and resourcefulness, by the perpetual cycle of challenge and response created by new ideas, new patterns of trade, new sources of competition, new technologies, new customers in the rapidly changing conditions of newly emergent countries, is equally a continuing one.

No business can afford to stand still; *laissez-faire* has certainly never been a part of Reeves policy. The selfless determination of C. J. Wild had brought the firm safely through the hazards of the First World War; no less important a contribution had been that of A. G. Simmons, whose

Water-front at Benares, from 'Oriental Scenery'. Thomas Daniell (Water-colour. c. 1790)

St. Anne's Hill. J. M. W. Turner
(Water-colour illustration to Samuel Rogers' 'Poems'. c. 1830)

Petworth House interiors. J. M. W. Turner (Water-colour. c. 1830)

Rocky Landscape-Sunset. J. S. Cotman (Water-colour, executed in the paste medium. c. 1835-9)

courage and drive steered Reeves through the lean post-war years and the perils of the General Strike. 'A.G.' had directed the sales policies of the company since the death of C. J. Wild and many of his ideas, notably the temperablock, provided the substance of Reeves achievements in the educational field.

In 1945, it had become clear that in the schools the fashion for coloured chalks and the traditional transparent water-colour paint boxes was declining in favour of opaque water-colours. Reeves, looking backwards to their pioneer development of powder, and liquid tempera colours, provided for the change by adapting these two products to a more convenient use. They went further. Following a period of research and experimental production, they introduced two important new products in shrewd anticipation of the momentum the new demand would gather; tempodiscs, powder colours compressed into tablet form to fit into the individual paint box, and temperablocks, larger versions of the tempodisc, for use by groups of children working together in an art class. Both products are to be found in most art classes and schools today, more especially in the primary and secondary schools, along with 'Presafix', a fixative for pastels, charcoal, and other pigments used in mural painting, and a wide variety of colouring media devised by Reeves for all aspects of art and craftwork, ranging from painting on paper to the decoration of ceramics and fabrics.

Of these, temperablocks, invented and promoted by A. G. Simmons, represented the most popular and commercially successful product of the kind introduced to the market. Simmons's original inspiration had been to provide children with 'colour just like a block of blanco'; the level of demand sustained to the present day for Reeves temperablocks amply testifies to the acuteness of his vision and the thrust which he applied to their early sales.

[49]

In 1964, the firm produced an altogether new painting medium based on acrylic vinyl copolymer, the resultant fast-drying polymer colours, contained in transparent plastic tubes for ease of identification, being applicable to all non-oily surfaces. There is now a division in the company for the exclusive production of pigment dispersions for colouring fibre-glass and various plastics, such as are used for motor-car bodies, boats, kitchen and bathroom fittings; such as it is anticipated will commonly be used in the form of reinforced or structural plastics in the building and structural industries.

Recently the four remaining London retail shops, controlled by Reeves retail subsidiary, Clifford Milburn Ltd., have been substantially reorganised and re-designed, and in conformity with the demands of the modern picture-buying public the Kensington shop, in particular, is currently stocked with original paintings as well as reproductions.

In commemorating the two hundred years of their continued existence, Reeves and Sons, as represented by management and staff alike, will in their own experience have witnessed a remarkable change in their company's status. In 1955 Reeves and Sons might fairly have been described as an old-established family business making art materials in the London area, with a growing export trade and a warehouse outlet in Canada. Today they are an international group of companies stemming from the same parent body, with subsidiaries operating all over the world, trading in a range of products far in excess of that envisaged even a decade ago. It is a proud transformation which would have offered sterling satisfaction to the staunch figures of earlier days. Like all Victorians the Reeves and the Wilds were hard workers. Capital for developing enterprises was hard to come by, and the greatest caution and calculation, not to say some little personal sacrifice, was required to finance a growing business. The energy and resourcefulness that had then to be applied by the business man, merchant, and factory owner was out of all proportion to the effort required by his modern counterpart in the performance of much the same duties. Since there were no telephones all communication had to be established either by letter or by travel. Since there were no typewriters everything had to be painfully written out by hand. Every successive step taken was in the nature of a pioneer experiment. It is well to remember that such difficulties as these attended something like three-quarters of Reeves full term of existence, if only to derive from them added vigour for the fresh difficulties that must inevitably lie ahead.

It would take a bold man and one with more detailed knowledge of the subject than the present writer enjoys to distinguish between the contribution made to the artist's development by the colourmen's successive innovations and the spur given to the colourmen by the evolving demands of the creative genius. It has been said that the essence of history is not so much the passage of events but the reactions of people to those events as they took place. That a continuous inter-action has existed between the stylistic metamorphoses of the artist and the technical advancement of the colour-making industry cannot be denied.

One would be on safer ground, however, to confine oneself to an appreciation of what the artists' colourman's contribution has been to the spread of art as both a professional and amateur accomplishment. On this score, and particularly on the evidence of the past hundred years, their contribution has been immense, not only as regards the removal of so many practical difficulties affecting the painter's task, which in turn has in itself served both to extend the horizons and enhance the popularity of all branches of pictorial art, but in the field of art education. In both these departments, as well as in many others, the achievements of Reeves and Sons rank supreme.

[51]